BIG PICTURE PRESS

First published in the UK in 2018 by Big Picture Press,
an imprint of Bonnier Books UK,
The Plaza, 535 King's Road, London, SW10 0SZ
www.templarco.co.uk/big-picture-press
www.bonnierbooks.co.uk

ISBN 978-1-78370-893-2

This book was typeset in Gill Sans and Mrs Green
The illustrations in this book are digital engravings.

Expert consultant: Dr Jonathan Tennant
Written by Lily Murray
Designed by Winsome d'Abreu, Wendy Bartlet and Marty Cleary
Edited by Isobel Boston and Tasha Percy

Printed in China

Welcome
to the
Museum

ENTER HERE

Dinosaurium

Illustrated by CHRIS WORMELL

Written by LILY MURRAY

BPP

Entrance

Welcome to Dinosaurium

This book is laid out like a museum, with lots of rooms to explore. It will transport you millions of years back in time to discover the largest and most ferocious land animals that ever lived – the dinosaurs. Marvel at all kinds of extraordinary species, from tiny feathered killers to giant plant-eaters that shook the Earth as they walked.

Even though the last dinosaurs lived millions of years ago, we know more about them now than ever before. They were first discovered in 1824 and in the last 30 years, more than half of all known species have been named. Palaeontologists (scientists who study fossils) are constantly making new discoveries and museums all around the world are adding to their collections.

As you enter this museum, you will tour galleries that reveal how dinosaurs lived and how they changed over time. Discover the amazing variety of species and find out what the dinosaurs ate, how they moved, where they lived and how they fought. See for yourself how dinosaurs evolved from their earliest forms and read the astonishing story of how they eventually evolved into birds. Enter here to explore the dinosaur kingdom in all its glory.

What is a Dinosaur?

Dinosaurs were a group of prehistoric reptiles that walked the Earth for 165 million years during a time called the Mesozoic era.

To begin with, they were scaly, two-legged creatures, but over time they developed into a spectacular variety of species – from fierce killers like *Tyrannosaurus rex* to gigantic plant-eaters like *Brachiosaurus*. They all lived on land, laid eggs and, like mammals, walked with their legs straight underneath their bodies. So far, scientists know of around 900 different species of dinosaur, but exciting new discoveries are being made all the time.

Scientists divide dinosaurs into two main groups. The first group are the saurischians, or 'lizard-hipped' dinosaurs, including meat-eaters called theropods and long-necked dinosaurs called sauropods. The second group are the ornithischians, or 'bird-hipped' dinosaurs. They include all the other plant-eaters.

Just under 66 million years ago, the reign of the dinosaurs came to a sudden end. Scientists believe this was caused by a giant asteroid, a large rock from space, falling from space and crashing into the Earth. More than half of the world's animals were wiped out, but one group of theropod dinosaurs found a way to survive. These two-legged flying animals still live among us today: we know them as birds. Incredibly, they all share links to the mighty theropod dinosaurs of the past.

─────────────── *Key to plate* ───────────────

1: **Saurischians (lizard-hipped)**
a) *Coelophysis bauri*
A theropod
Late Triassic, North America
Length: 3m; Weight: 25kg

b) *Brachiosaurus altithorax*
A sauropod
Late Jurassic, North America
Length: 25m; Weight: 28,000kg

2: **Ornithischians (bird-hipped)**
a) *Iguandon bernissartensis*
An ornithopod
Early Cretaceous, Europe
Length: 10m; Weight: 3200kg

b) *Euplocephalus tutus*
 An ankylosaur
Late Cretaceous, Canada
Length: 6m; Weight: 2500kg

c) *Diabloceratops eatoni*
A ceratopsian
Late Cretaceous, USA
Length: 5.5m; Weight: 2000kg

4

The Triassic Period

The first dinosaurs appeared during the Triassic – the first of three periods that make up the Mesozoic era. During the Triassic, the Earth looked very different to how it does today. Most of the continents were joined together in a single 'supercontinent' known as Pangaea. The world was hot and dry, and huge deserts stretched across much of the land.

Just before the Triassic, most of the animals on Earth had been killed by a huge extinction. The Triassic period saw the return of life on land, with both the early ancestors of mammals and dinosaurs appearing for the first time. On higher, wetter ground, and along the coasts, there were forests of conifer trees, as well as mosses and ferns, and many different types of insects. The largest animals were the archosaurs (early reptiles) and mammal-like reptiles, known as therapsids.

In the middle of the Triassic, the first dinosaurs appeared, followed by winged reptiles, as well as tiny shrewlike creatures – our earliest mammal ancestors.

Key to plate

1: *Postosuchus*
Length: 5m; Weight: 680kg
An archosaur and a top predator, *Postosuchus* was fast-moving and may have walked on two legs.

2: 'Fanged pterosaur'
Wingspan: 1.3m;
Weight: uncertain
This small pterosaur preyed on insects and tiny ancient ancestors of crocodiles.

3: Bennettitales
Bennettitales were palm-like plants with tough leaves and woody trunks.

4: *Araucarioxylon arizonicum*
These conifer trees covered much of North America in the Late Triassic. Their closest relative today is the monkey puzzle tree.

5: Horsetails
These fast-growing, rush-like plants were an important food source for the plant-eaters of the day.

6: *Morganucodon*
Length: 13cm; Weight: 27–89g
Morguanucodon was an early mammal ancestor which laid eggs and was most likely nocturnal (active at night).

The Jurassic Period

The Triassic period ended just as it had begun, with another mass extinction that wiped out half the species on the planet. For much of the Triassic, dinosaurs had lived alongside other reptiles, but now they were gone, the dinosaurs became the most dominant animals on land.

During the Jurassic, Pangaea broke up into two major landmasses. As the continent split apart, seas flooded the land and Earth's climate became much wetter and milder. Plant life flourished and spread across the land in thick forests of ferns, conifers and palm-like cycads. This rich plant growth supported animal life of different kinds, ranging from tiny mammals that scurried along the branches to the first birds, which evolved from small, meat-eating dinosaurs.

The Jurassic period saw the appearance of powerful meat-eating dinosaurs, gigantic marine life and huge plant-eaters that shook the Earth as they walked.

―――――――――― *Key to plate* ――――――――――

1: Tianyulong confuciusi
Length: 70cm; Weight: 800g
A small, plant-eating dinosaur, *Tianyulong* is famous for having a feather-like fuzz along its back.

2: Mongolarachne jurassica
Body length: 1.65cm;
Leg length: 5.82cm
Mongolarachne was a spider covered in feathery hair. It was probably most active at night,

hiding in caves or the cracks in trees and rocks during the day.

3: Dicksonia
Dicksonia was a type of tree fern with an upright trunk.

4: Williamsonia
Williamsonia was a plant with thin, woody stems, fern-like leaves and long flowers.

5: Ginkgo
A tree with a single seed on the end of little stalks and leaves with rounded, wavy edges. One species of *Ginkgo* still survives in the wild today, in China.

6: Juramaia sinensis
Length: 7–10cm; Weight: 15g
Juramaia was a small, shrew-like mammal that hunted for insects among the ferns.

The Cretaceous Period

The Cretaceous was the last and the longest period of the Mesozoic era and was a time of huge change. As the continents continued to drift apart, rising seas covered large parts of the land to form smaller continents. Flowering plants appeared for the first time, along with the insects that fed on them.

There were more dinosaur species in the Cretaceous than at any other time. Species were evolving differently on each landmass, and as a result the dinosaurs were evolving into a dazzling variety of forms. There were new types of plant-eating dinosaurs appearing and also fearsome meat-eaters, including the infamous *Tyrannosaurus rex*.

The skies were filled with flying reptiles known as pterosaurs and many different species of birds, while ichthyosaurs and plesiosaurs swam in the seas.

Then, at the end of the Cretaceous, came the extinction that wiped out the dinosaurs and 75 per cent of all animals and plant life. The 'Age of Reptiles' was over.

—————————————————— *Key to plate* ——————————————————

1: Minmi paravertebra
Length: 3m; Weight: 300kg
A small, plant-eating ankylosaur from Australia, *Minmi* ate the seeds and fruit of flowering plants, along with ferns.

2: Muttaburrasaurus langdoni
Length: 8m; Weight: 2800kg
Muttaburrasaurus was an ornithopod dinosaur with rows of teeth for grinding up plants.

3: Mythunga camara
Wingspan: 4.7m;
Weight: uncertain
Mythunga was a large fish-eating pterosaur.

4: **Conifer forest**
These forests covered much of Australia in the Cretaceous, especially along the coasts.

5: **Flowering plants**
The first flowering plants appeared in the Early Cretaceous period.

6: Nanantius eos
Wingspan: 35cm; Weight: 80g
A bird from the Early Cretaceous, *Nanantius* was about the size of a blackbird. It probably fed on small fish and other tiny sea creatures.

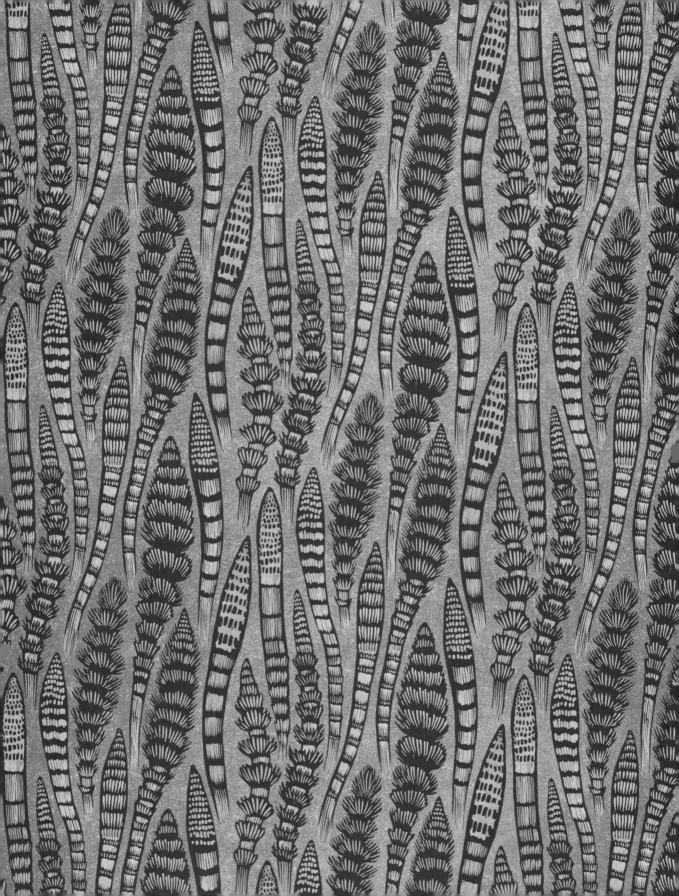

Gallery 1

Sauropodomorphs

Sauropodomorphs

Early Sauropodomorphs

Sauropods

Sauropodomorphs

This group of dinosaurs includes the sauropods, the largest animals to walk the Earth, and their early relatives, which were among the very first dinosaurs. The sauropodomorphs were saurischian, or 'lizard-hipped' dinosaurs, with small heads, long necks and long tails for balance. Their fossils have been found all over the world and they lived in many different habitats, from swamps to deserts.

To begin with, the sauropodomorphs were small and walked on two legs. Over time, however, they grew larger and larger, and their increasing size forced them to spread their weight across four pillar-like legs.

As a group, they were incredibly successful, becoming the top plant-eaters for much of the Mesozoic era. Most species had leaf-shaped teeth, which could easily slice through plants, but they could not grind up their food. Instead, they swallowed small stones, known as gastroliths, to help them digest tough plant matter.

The largest sauropodomorphs have come to symbolise the meaning of the word 'dinosaur' in the popular imagination – unimaginably huge animals that were taller than buildings and longer than buses.

Key to plate

1: Brachiosaurus altithorax
Late Jurassic, North America
Length: 25m; Weight: 28,000kg
When its fossils were discovered in 1900, Brachiosaurus took the record of the largest dinosaur. Bigger dinosaurs have since been discovered, but it is still one of the tallest known species.

Brachiosaurus had a body like a giraffe, with a long neck and front legs that may have sprawled outwards. It would have used its neck to reach leaves on high branches. In order to survive, it needed to eat up to 120kg of plants and leaves a day.

2: Brachiosaurus skull
This dinosaur had a wide skull with thick jawbones, and 52 spoon-shaped teeth, well-suited to stripping leaves from branches. Its nostrils would have filled the large spaces on the top of its head.

Early Sauropodomorphs

The oldest known sauropodomorphs date from the dawn of the dinosaurs. They first appeared in the Triassic period, around 225 to 200 million years ago. These dinosaurs were the early relatives of huge giants like *Diplodocus*, but they were much smaller, walked on two legs and probably ate both plants and animals. They had large thumb claws for pulling down branches to eat, and for defending themselves against attack.

From the Late Triassic to the Early Jurassic, they were the most common plant-eating dinosaurs of their day and their fossils have been found on every continent. However, by the Mid-Jurassic they began to die out, possibly as their relatives, the larger sauropods, began to compete with them for food.

───────────────── *Key to plate* ─────────────────

1: Massospondylus carinatus
Early Jurassic, Zimbabwe
Length: 4m; Weight: 135kg
A long-necked dinosaur, *Massospondylus* probably used its huge thumb claws to tear off branches from trees.

2: Plateosaurus engelhardti
Late Triassic, Europe
Length: 10m; Weight: 4000kg

Plateosaurus is one of the best known dinosaurs from Europe. Hundreds of their fossils have been found together in one place, suggesting they may have lived in herds.

3: Thecodontosaurus antiquus
Late Triassic, England
Length: 2.5m; Weight: 40kg
This dinosaur was thought to

be a 'dwarf' species that lived only on islands. It was the fourth dinosaur ever to be named.

4: Riojasaurus incertus
Late Triassic, Argentina
Length: 6.6m; Weight: 800kg
With its large body and bulky legs, *Riojasaurus* was a slow-moving animal that was unable to rear up on its back legs.

Sauropods

The sauropods were the giants of the dinosaur world. There were species as tall as buildings and at their heaviest they weighed close to 100,000kg – 16 times heavier than an African elephant. But *how* did they get to be so big?

Sauropods were plant-eaters, and one of their key features was their long necks, which allowed them to browse for food at the very tops of tall trees. They could eat quickly too, swallowing their food without chewing, and they were able to digest enormous amounts of plant matter in their huge stomachs. They had long tails and supported their immense weight on four pillar-like legs.

Sauropods walked the Earth for over 100 million years. They died out at the end of the Cretaceous, and no land animal since has ever come close to their size.

―――――――――――――――――――― *Key to plate* ――――――――――――――――――――

1: Mamenchisaurus hochuanensis
Late Jurassic, China
Length: 25m; Weight: 36,000kg
This dinosaur is famous for its extraordinarily long neck, which took up half the length of its body.

2: Diplodocus carnegii
Late Jurassic, USA
Length: 28m; Weight: 18,000kg
Diplodocus was one of the longest-known dinosaurs. It is thought to have swung its tail fast enough to make a loud noise, in order to scare off predators.

3: Nigersaurus taqueti
Mid-Cretaceous, Niger
Length: 9m; Weight: 2000kg
This dinosaur's incredibly wide jaws were filled with around 200 needle-shaped teeth. It probably fed by swinging its neck from side to side, clipping off plant matter as it went.

4: Amargasaurus cazaui
Early Cretaceous, Argentina
Length: 13m; Weight: 4000kg
Amargasaurus was instantly recognisable by the rows of forked spines on its back, which were probably used for defence.

Gallery 2

Theropods

Theropods

The theropods were the killers of the dinosaur world. Most were meat-eaters that walked on two legs, and had sharp claws for grabbing prey and curved teeth for cutting flesh.

They first appeared in the Late Triassic and were saurischian, or 'lizard-hipped' dinosaurs. By the Jurassic period, theropods had become the most powerful predators on land and remained so for 100 million years, right up until the end of the Cretaceous.

All modern birds are, in fact, descended from small, flightless theropods. From the Jurassic period some theropods were beginning to resemble birds with beaks and arm feathers that looked a lot like wings. We now know that some species displayed bird-like behaviour too – building nests and protecting their eggs.

Theropod fossils have been found all around the world, from Asia to Antarctica. These fossil finds show the incredible range of theropod forms, from the crow-sized *Microraptor* to giants like *Tyrannosaurus* and *Spinosaurus*.

Key to plate

1: Coelophysis bauri
Late Triassic, North America
Length: 3m; Weight: 25kg
This dinosaur was first discovered in 1881 and is one of the best known theropods from the Late Triassic period. It had many theropod features, including hands for grasping prey and sharp teeth and claws.

Coelophysis was a dog-sized dinosaur, that probably fed on fish, insects and small reptiles. In 1947, over 1000 individuals were found together, suggesting that it may have hunted in packs.

2: Coelophysis bauri skeleton
This shows the position of a fossil *Coelophysis* from Arizona, USA. You can clearly see the three large toes on its feet that it used for walking, the small fourth toe and its long S-shaped neck.

1

Allosauroidea

Allosauridae were medium to large carnivores and were the most successful hunters of the Late Jurassic. Their most famous member, *Allosaurus*, ruled the American Midwest, equipped with its knife-like teeth, powerful claws and long, muscular legs. It would have hunted stegosaurs, ornithopods and even the enormous sauropods, which were up to ten times its size.

However, by the Cretaceous period, *Allosaurus* and its close relatives were dying out, and a new group of fearsome predators had arrived on the scene – Carcharodontosauridae. This group of dinosaurs included some of the largest land predators ever, which were all equal in size or even larger than *Tyrannosaurus rex. Carcharodontosaurus*, after which the group

is named, was twice the weight of an elephant, with sharp, serrated teeth and a body the length of a bus.

Key to plate

1: Allosaurus fragilis
Late Jurassic, USA
Length: 8.5m; Weight: 1700kg
Allosaurus was a typical theropod, with an S-shaped neck, a large skull and long tail. It was known to be a fearsome predator; and evidence of *Allosaurus* bite marks have been found on a *Stegosaurus* neck

plate. However, *Allosaurus'* bites weren't strong enough to crush bone. Instead, it probably made slashing bites at its prey in an attempt to weaken it.

2: Carcharodontosaurus saharicus skull
Mid-Cretaceous, Africa
Length: 13m; Weight: 6000kg

Named after *Carcharodon*, the scientific name for the Great White Shark, *Carcharodontosaurus* means 'sharp-toothed' and its skull shows why – it was full of enormous, serrated teeth up to 20cm long.

1

Spinosaurus

Longer and heavier than the formidable *Tyrannosaurus rex*, *Spinosaurus* may have been the largest land predator of all time. This mighty theropod had a long, narrow snout and a huge sail on its back, which stood over 2m tall.

The sail itself was made up of a series of spines attached to *Spinosaurus'* backbone. Scientists think it was used for display, and may have been brightly coloured, like the fins of some reptiles alive today.

Spinosaurus' long snout was filled with pointed teeth, which were perfectly

suited to spearing fish. It probably spent much of its life wading in water, hunting for prey. It didn't only eat fish, however. *Spinosaurus* could also run very fast, and its diet may have included land animals as well as huge fish and sharks.

Key to plate

1: Spinosaurus aegyptiacus
Mid-Cretaceous, Egypt
Length: 18m; Weight: 9000kg
Spinosaurus had many features that suggest it was well-suited to a watery life. Its nostrils were high up on its snout, meaning it would have been able to breathe even when its body was mostly underwater. *Spinosaurus'* wide, flat claws and feet would also have been perfect for paddling.

This dinosaur was able to carve out a niche for itself alongside other theropods of the day, hunting for fish and other marine and shore-dwelling prey.

1a

1b

1c

1d

Feathered Killers

For many years, the meat-eating hunters of the dinosaur world were thought to be enormous, scaly beasts, but our understanding of them is quickly changing. One group of dinosaurs, called Coelurosauria, are now believed to have had a type of feathery covering at some point in their lives. This group includes giant theropods, such as *Tyrannosaurus rex*, as well as smaller troodons and raptors.

The discovery of feathers on non-flying dinosaurs suggests that feathers may have first evolved for reasons other than flight. They could have been used for camouflage, for warmth, to line nests and even to attract mates.

This group of dinosaurs has also revealed another astonishing secret: during the Jurassic period, small theropod dinosaurs began evolving into birds. In fact, certain theropod dinosaurs and birds have so many features in common that many scientists call birds 'avian dinosaurs'.

Key to plate

1: **Evolution of feathers**
a) Simple, hollow barb. First appeared 150 million years ago
b) Hair-like tufts of downy fuzz, as found on the dinosaur *Dilong*
c) A feather with a central shaft,

as found on *Sinornithosaurus*
d) Modern flight feather

2: Dilong paradoxus
Early Cretaceous, China
Length: 2m; Weight: 10kg

This dinosaur was a small, early relative of *Tyrannosaurus*. It was covered in fluffy down, and its discovery showed that it wasn't just the small, bird-like dinosaurs that had feathers.

Tyrannosaurus

Tyrannosaurus was a ferocious killer that ruled western North America during the Late Cretaceous period. Although larger meat-eating dinosaurs have since been discovered, *Tyrannosaurus* remains one of most famous dinosaurs.

Its full name, *Tyrannosaurus rex*, means 'tyrant lizard king', and is well deserved. Its short, deep skull allowed it to a generate powerful bite forces, and unlike many other predators of the time, it was able to crunch through the protective plates of armoured dinosaurs. This meant that it would have been able to attack and kill almost any animal it ran into.

As *Tyrannosaurus* is known from a number of fossils, scientists have been able to build up a very detailed picture of its life. We know that it grew extremely fast, and was fully grown by its early twenties. It may have been covered in downy fuzz, or feathers, and could well have lived and hunted in packs.

Young tyrannosaurs would have been able to run quite fast, but as they grew older and heavier, they slowed, and may have scavenged on dead animals rather than hunting live prey.

Key to plate

1: Tyrannosaurus rex
Late Cretaceous,
North America
Length: 12m; Weight: 6000kg
Tyrannosaurus had a typical theropod shape. Its enormous head was on the end of an S-shaped neck and it had a long, heavy tail for balance. Scientists are still unsure what *Tyrannosaurus* used its short arms and two clawed fingers for, but it was most likely for gripping on to prey whilst feeding.

Oviraptorosaurs

This group of bird-like dinosaurs were extremely unusual-looking. They had short skulls with parrot-like beaks, and many had bony crests on their heads. Some were as small as turkeys, while others grew to an impressive 8m long. Many species had wing feathers, and some had short tails that may have ended in a fan of feathers.

The name 'oviraptorosaur' means 'egg thief', because an early fossil find appeared to show an oviraptor raiding another dinosaur's nest. However, on closer examination the scientists discovered that the oviraptorosaur was in fact sitting on its own eggs to keep them warm, just like a modern bird.

Oviraptorosaurs probably ate both plants and animals. One fossil was found with the bones of a baby dinosaur in its stomach, while others have been found containing small stones, called gastroliths, similar to those used by animals today to help grind up plants.

Key to plate

1: Gigantoraptor erlianensis
Late Cretaceous, Mongolia
Length: 8m; Weight: 1400kg
As tall as a giraffe, *Gigantoraptor* is the largest known beaked dinosaur. If it was feathered, it would have been one of the largest feathered animals of all time.

2: Anzu wyliei
Late Cretaceous, N. America
Length: 3m; Weight: 225kg
The discovery of *Anzu* suggests some oviraptorosaurs may have eaten eggs after all – small prongs of bone in its mouth match those found in today's egg-eating snakes.

3: Heyuannia huangi
Late Cretaceous, China
Length: 1.5m; Weight: 20kg
Heyuannia's fossils were found alongside thousands of eggs. Incredibly, the colour of the eggs was preserved, so we know that they were a blue-green colour.

Therizinosaurus

For many years *Therizinosaurus* did nothing but puzzle scientists. It was first discovered in 1948, in the Gobi Desert in Mongolia, but its remains were initially mistaken for a turtle-like lizard. It was only after another therizinosaur was discovered in 1973 that it was finally recognised as a dinosaur.

Therizinosaurus was a theropod, but unlike the rest of the group, it only ate plants. With its heavy body, pot belly and short legs, it would have been much too slow to catch prey. Instead, its jaws were full of small leaf-shaped teeth that would have been better adapted for eating plants.

Scientists now think *Therizinosaurus* used its curved claws to pull leaves from branches, much like modern sloths do today. But that might not have been all they were used for – *Therizinosaurus* shared its habitat with *Tarbosaurus bataar*, a close relative of *Tyrannosaurus*, so its slashing curved claws may also have been used as a vital means of defence.

Key to plate

1: Therizinosaurus cheloniformis
Late Cretaceous, Mongolia
Length: 10m; Weight: 5000kg
With its 90cm-long curved claws, *Therizinosaurus* holds the record for the dinosaur with the longest claws of all time. This species is known only from an incomplete skeleton, including parts of its forelimbs, back legs, ribs and mighty arms and claws. It is shown here covered in feathers, following the discovery that another similar species, *Beipiaosaurus*, was covered in a coat of long, feather-like fibres.

1

Troodon

At first, *Troodon* was only known from a single, curved tooth, found in Montana, USA, in 1856. Although it was one of the first dinosaur finds in North America, the tooth was initially thought to have come from a lizard. However, we now know that *Troodon* was a theropod, and belonged to a group of dinosaurs which may well be the ancestors of modern birds.

Troodon was a fast-running, skillful hunter. Its large eyes were at the front of its skull, which meant they were perfectly positioned for focusing and tracking down prey, even in dim light. One ear was a little higher than the other, just like owls today, which suggests that they may have used their sharp hearing to find prey at night. It is thought they hunted small mammals, lizards and insects, although a larger plant-eating dinosaur, *Edmontosaurus*, has also been found with *Troodon* bite marks, suggesting they may have hunted in packs to bring down larger animals.

Troodon is thought to have been among the most intelligent dinosaurs. It had an unusually large brain for its body size, and it is believed to have been as intelligent as modern birds.

One of the most exciting *Troodon* finds was in 1984, when a nest of 19 eggs was discovered in Montana, USA. Each egg still had a tiny skeleton inside.

─────────────── *Key to plate* ───────────────

1: Troodonosus formosus
Late Cretaceous, N. America
Length: 2m; Weight: 50kg
Troodon lived during the Late
Cretaceous period, 66 to 75 million years ago. It had long hindlimbs and large, sickle-shaped claws on the second toes, which it raised off the ground while running.

1

Dromaeosaurs

A family of fast-running, feathered predators, dromaeosaurs first appeared in the Middle Jurassic, but really flourished in the Cretaceous period, when they spread across the globe. They were among the most birdlike of dinosaurs, with some species even folding their arms against their bodies, just like the wings of modern birds. Unlike modern birds, however, they had large hands with three long fingers ending in sharp claws.

Within the dromaeosaur family, there was a group known as 'true dramaeosaurs' or 'raptors'. These were larger than the others, and the biggest, *Utahraptor*, grew to the size of a polar bear. The raptors had claws on their second toes, that could have been used as deadly weapons to attack much larger dinosaurs.

A discovery in 2001 shed further light on possible dromaeosaur behaviour. Up to six *Utahraptor* fossils were found with the remains of a large plant-eating dinosaur in a block of sandstone. It's possible that the *Utrahraptors* were trying to attack the dinosaur when they became trapped in quicksand. If this is correct, then it proves that dromaeosaurs were pack-hunting killers.

─────────────────────── *Key to plate* ───────────────────────

1: Bambiraptor feinbergi
Late Cretaceous, USA
Length: 1m; Weight: 2kg
Bambiraptor was a small dromaeosaur with long back legs, suggesting it could have been a fast runner. It also had a large brain for its body size.

2: Deinonychus antirrhopus
Mid-Cretaceous, USA
Length: 3.4m; Weight: 73kg
Deinonychus' name means 'terrible claw', due to the deadly claws on its toes, which it used to slice open its prey. It also had powerful jaws filled with blade-like teeth.

3: Dakotaraptor steini
Late Cretaceous, USA
Length: 5.5m; Weight: 200kg
Dakotaraptor was a giant raptor, second only in size to *Utahraptor*. Although it was too large for flight, it is the largest known dinosaur with wings.

Dino Birds

In Liaoning Province, in northeastern China, lies one of the world's most fascinating fossil sites. During the Early Cretaceous period, 130 to 110 million years ago, volcanic eruptions in the area covered the plants and animals that lived there with ash and mud. This preserved them in astonishing detail. In the 1990s, scientists uncovered dinosaur fossils from the site that were unlike anything the world had ever seen before. For the first time, scientists were able to look at the soft body parts of dinosaurs, even the contents of their stomachs, and here was the first proof that dinosaurs had feathers.

These 'dino birds', as they became known, lived in a warm, wet forest, dotted with lakes. They would have lived alongside giant insects, shrew-like creatures and mammals the size of dogs. There were frogs and turtles, similar to those around today. Early birds flitted from branch to branch, while strange feathered dinosaurs climbed the trees.

─── *Key to plate* ───

1: Sinornithosaurus millenii
Length: 90cm; Weight: 1.5kg
This little feathered dinosaur may be the first known venomous dinosaur, paralysing its prey with its bite. It would have swooped down on its prey from low-hanging tree branches.

2: Confuciusornis sanctus
Length: 50cm; Weight: 1kg
Around the size of a pigeon,

Confuciusornis is the earliest-known bird without teeth. It could fly, but unlike modern birds it still had clawed fingers on its wings.

3: Sinosauropteryx prima
Length: 1.7m; Weight: 0.55kg
In 1996, *Sinosauropteryx* became the first non-bird dinosaur discovered with feathers. Because it was only distantly related to birds, the

discovery suggests that many theropod dinosaurs were feathered rather than scaly.

4: Mei long
Length: 40cm; Weight: 0.4kg
A duck-sized relative of *Troodon, Mei* was found with its beak tucked under its wing, just like a roosting bird.

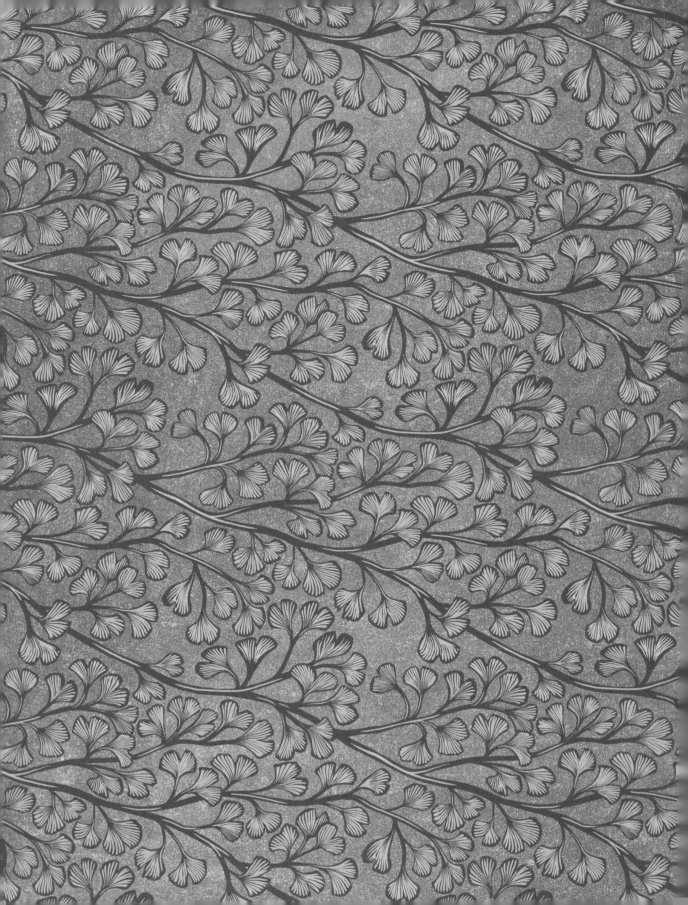

Gallery 3

Ornithopods

Ornithopods
Iguanodon
Hadrosaurs
Egg Mountain

Ornithopods

The ornithopods were ornithischian, or 'bird-hipped' dinosaurs, that included some of the most successful plant eaters of the Mesozoic era. They all had horny beaks, but were not covered in armour plating like other ornithischians.

Early ornithopods were small and swift and moved on two legs, while later species were often larger and better adapted to grazing on all fours. They first appeared in the Mid-Jurassic period and lasted until the very end of the Cretaceous. One of the secrets of their success was their powerful teeth and

jaws, which were well-adapted to grinding up tough plant food.

Their fossils have been found on every continent and, by the end of the Cretaceous, there were more species of ornithopod than any other dinosaur.

─────────────────────────── *Key to plate* ───────────────────────────

1: *Tenontosaurus tilletti*
(being attacked by a pack of *Deinonychus*)
Early Cretaceous, N. America
Length: 8m; Weight: 1500kg
This ornithopod would have been able to walk on all fours as well as on its back legs. It had a stiff, bony tail, which made up

over half the length of its body. Like other ornithopods, it would have fed on plants.

Scientists think *Tenotosaurus* may have been hunted by a bird-like theropod called *Deinonychus*, as many *Tenontosaurus* fossils have been found with those of *Deinonychus*.

One young *Tenontosaurus* was even found with *Deinonychus* bite marks in its bones. However, it is not known if the bite marks were made when the *Tenontosaurus* was alive, or if the *Deinonychus* was scavenging on the bones after the creature had died.

Iguanodon

In 1822, English fossil enthusiast Gideon Mantell found a scattering of fossil teeth that seemed to belong to a giant lizard. He named the creature *Iguanodon*, because of the similarity of the teeth to an iguana's. At first it was thought that *Iguanodon* was a lumbering four-legged beast with a spike on the tip of its nose. It was only in 1878 that scientists were able to work out what this dinosaur actually looked like, when 30 *Iguanadon* skeletons were discovered in a coal mine in Belgium. Many skeletons were nearly complete, and scientists were able to work out how the bones fitted together.

We now know *Iguanodon* to have been a bulky beast, built for walking, not running. It spent most of its time on all fours, browsing for food, and its spike was on its thumb, not its nose. *Iguanodon*'s story shows that our understanding of dinosaurs is always developing as exciting new discoveries come to light.

Key to plate

1: Iguanodon bernissartensis
Early Cretaceous, Europe
Length: 10m; Weight: 3200kg
Although it spent most of its time on all fours, *Iguanodon* could also move around on its back legs. Like other ornithopods, it had a bony,

toothless beak and closely packed teeth for grinding up tough plants.

2: Iguanodon hand
Iguanodon had three middle fingers on each hand and a grasping little finger used to

forage for food. The purpose of the *Iguanodon*'s thumb spike is still uncertain. Some scientists believe it was used for defence, while others claim it was used to break open large seeds and fruit.

Hadrosaurs

For millions of years, this group of broad-beaked dinosaurs were one of the world's most successful plant-eaters. Also known as 'duckbills', they were the cows of their day, moving in large herds across the Mesozoic landscape, stripping back low-growing plants with their teeth, which were constantly being replaced. Their fossils have been found all over Europe, Asia and North America.

Their flat, duck-like beaks were perfect for clipping off leaves, and they developed incredibly powerful teeth and jaws. It is thought they lived mainly on a diet of conifers, eating both the tough pine needles and the cones.

Many hadrosaurs had extravagant head crests. Some species are thought to have blown through their crests to make low, booming sounds, to call to other members of their herds.

Key to plate

1: Parasaurolophus walkeri
Late Cretaceous, N. America
Length: 9m; Weight: 2500kg
This dinosaur's huge crest was filled with twisting hollow tubes that connected to its nostrils. It would have blown up through its nostrils to make sounds to call to its herd.

2: Tsintaosaurus spinorhinus
Late Cretaceous, China
Length: 10m; Weight: 3000kg
The size of an elephant, *Tsintaosaurus* is also known as the 'unicorn dinosaur' for its horn-shaped crest.

3: Lambeosaurus lambei
Late Cretaceous, Canada
Length: 9m; Weight: 2500kg
The shape of this dinosaur's crest is known to have changed as the animal aged.

4: Edmontosaurus regalis
Late Cretaceous, N. America
Length: 14m; Weight: 4000kg
Instead of a crest, this dinosaur had a soft comb on its head, like that of a cockerel. It was probably used for display.

5: Saurolophus angustirostris
Late Cretaceous, Mongolia
Length: 12m; Weight: 3500kg
Saurolophus was the most common hadrosaur in Asia. Its spike-like crest was made up entirely of its nasal bone.

6: Corythosaurus casuarius
Late Cretaceous, Canada
Lenght: 9m; Weight: 2500kg
Like *Parasaurolophus*, *Corythosaurus* is thought to have used its crest for display and to make loud calls to its herd.

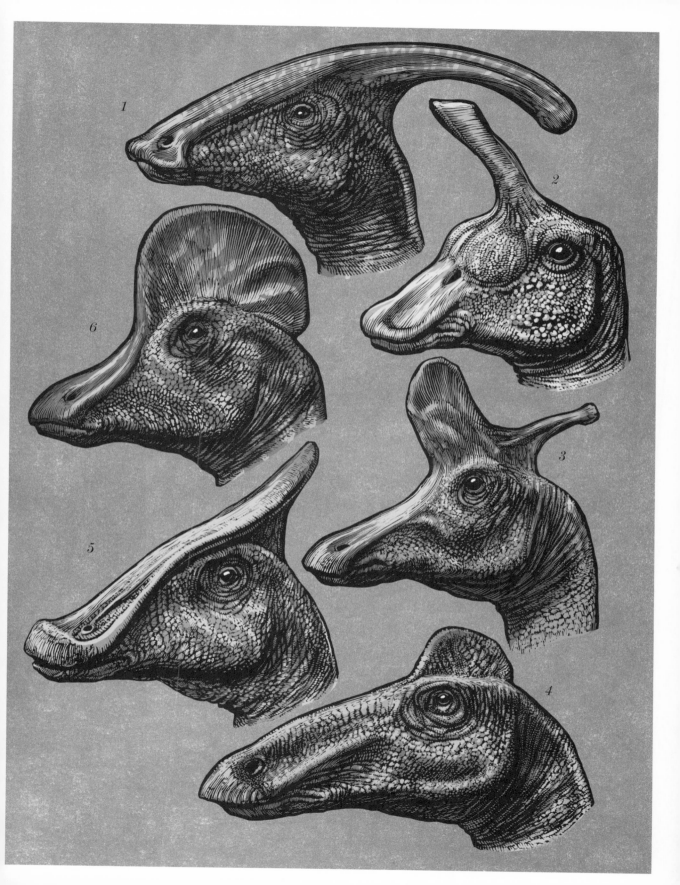

Egg Mountain

Around 77 million years ago, deep in the Rocky Mountains of Montana, USA, a herd of *Maiasaura* came to make their nests and lay eggs. Many would never hatch. Instead, they were covered by a cloud of volanic ash, perfectly preserving them for millions of years.

This fossil site, known as 'Egg Mountain', was discovered in 1979 and proved, for the first time, that dinosaurs looked after their young. The site contained hundreds of *Maiasaura* fossils, from adults to babies, along with bowl-shaped nests filled with eggs. Scientists also found plants that had been regurgitated (chewed, digested and then brought back up), which may be evidence of parents bringing food to their young. Older nests were found in the layers of rock below, so it seems that herds of *Maiasaura* returned to the same place, year after year, to lay their eggs.

Key to plate

1: *Maiasaura peeblesorum*
Late Cretaceous, USA
Length: 9m; Weight: 3000kg
This hadrosaur's name means 'good mother lizard', as it was found caring for its young. A duck-billed dinosaur, *Maiasaura* was a herbivore, feeding on plants, leaves and berries. It is thought to have roamed the Cretaceous landscape in vast herds, 10,000 strong, before returning to its nesting sites.

2: Nest
Width: 1.8m
Maiasaura nests were bowl-shaped and were full of rotting plants. Too heavy to sit on the eggs themselves, *Maiasaura* would have used the heat from the rotting plants to keep their eggs warm. Each nest was about 7m apart, leaving just enough space for adult *Maiasaura* to tend to their eggs.

3: Eggs
Length: 15cm
The eggs were about the size of a grapefruit, with around 30 in each nest, arranged in a circle, or a spiral pattern.

4: Hatchling
Length: 40cm; Weight: 1kg
Tiny at birth, the hatchlings grew quickly, reaching adult size at the age of eight. They walked on two legs at first, then mostly on all fours as adults.

Gallery 4

Thyreophora

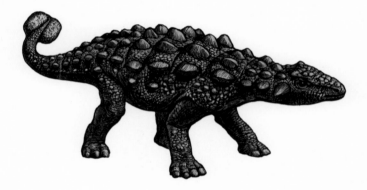

Thyreophorans

Stegosaurs

Ankylosaurs

Thyreophorans

This group of ornithischian dinosaurs lived from the Early Jurassic to the Late Cretaceous period. The name 'thyreophorans' means 'shield bearers', but they are more commonly known as 'armoured dinosaurs' because of their tough body armour, which they developed to protect themselves from the fearsome predators of the day.

Early thyreophorans were smaller and had much less body armour than those that came later in the Mesozoic. They had bony lumps in their skin, much like crocodiles today. These lumps were covered in keratin, the same material fingernails are made from, and were arranged in rows along the dinosaurs' back. Later thyreophorans, however, had large parts of their bodies covered in thick, bony plates, along with a dazzling variety of horns and spikes.

Despite their ferocious appearance, all thyreophorans were plant-eaters. They probably had hooflike claws on their feet and a horny beak, which would have been used to clip leaves from low-growing branches.

Thyreophorans are divided into two main groups – the stegosaurs, with their rows of plates and spines along their backs, and the more heavily armoured, tank-like ankylosaurs.

--- *Key to plate* ---

1: Scutellosaurus lawleri
Early Jurassic, USA
Length: 1.3m; Weight: 10kg
Scutellosaurus was a very early type of thyreophoran. It walked on two legs (almost all other thyreophorans walked on four) and was swift and agile, with a long tail for balance. However, it didn't have to rely on speed alone to escape from predators. Its name, meaning 'small shield lizard', reflects the fact that Scutellosaurus was covered in more than 300 bony lumps, which were strong enough to break a predator's teeth.

Stegosaurs

The stegosaurs were a distinctive-looking group of dinosaurs. To defend themselves against predators, they developed bony plates and spikes on their bodies. Some stegosaurs had spikes on their sides, to stop predators from getting too close, while others had spikes on their tails, which they could use as defensive weapons. Indeed, many predators' bones have been found with puncture holes that fit the shapes of these spikes.

The rows of bony plates along a stegosaur's back would have made the animal look bigger, but they were also covered in blood vessels. Stegosaurs could have pumped blood through these plates, blushing them red, possibly to attract mates or to warn off rivals.

Early stegosaurs were only about 3m long, but later forms could reach up to 9m or more. They were most common in the Mid to Late Jurassic, but had died out by the Early Cretaceous. Their fossils have been found all over the world.

--- *Key to plate* ---

1: Kentrosaurus aethiopicus
Late Jurassic, Tanzania
Length: 5m; Weight: 1000kg
The spikiest of the stegosaurs, *Kentrosaurus* had long spikes on its shoulders to protect itself from being attacked from the side. It could also swing its tail at high speeds to cause severe damage to attacking theropods.

2: Huayangosaurus taibaii
Middle Jurassic, China
Length: 4m; Weight: 850kg
An early stegosaur, and one of the smallest-known, *Huayangosaurus* had a wider skull than later stegosaurs, teeth at the front of its mouth and relatively long forelimbs.

3: Stegosaurus armatus
Late Jurassic, USA and Portugal
Length: 9m; Weight: 2000kg
Stegosaurus was the largest of the stegosaurs, with diamond-shaped plates along its back and a narrow skull. Its front legs were much longer than its back legs, which meant it wouldn't have been able to move very quickly.

1

Ankylosaurs

The ankylosaurs were among the most heavily armoured dinosaurs ever to walk the Earth. Some species had spear-like spines along their neck and back, while others had armoured heads. A few species were armed with another impressive weapon – a heavy club at the end of their tail. These tail clubs were made of several plates of bone joined together and could be swung at predators with bone-shattering force.

Bulky and heavy, ankylosaurs were probably slow-moving animals that fed on low-growing plants. Like other thyreophorans, they didn't chew their food, but slowly digested it in their huge stomachs.

The ankylosaurs lived from the Jurassic until the very end of the Cretaceous period, and they were among the last dinosaurs to walk the Earth.

Key to plate

1: Euoplocephalus tutus
Late Cretaceous, Canada
Length: 6m; Weight: 2500kg
Euoplocephalus was covered in thick, bony armour, except for parts of its legs and tail. It had powerful tail muscles, so it could swing its club from side to side, most likely at the breakable shin bones of advancing theropods.

2: Ankylosaurus magniventris
Late Cretaceous, N. America
Length: 7m; Weight: 3000kg
The largest of the ankylosaurs, *Ankylosaurus* was so heavily armoured that even its eyelids were covered in bony plates. It would have needed this extra protection to see off the predators of the day, which included *Tyrannosaurus rex*.

3: Sauropelta edwardsorum
Early Cretaceous, USA
Length: 5m; Weight: 1500kg
Sauropelta had enormous neck spines, as well as a covering of body armour. It lived in wide floodplains and possibly in herds, as the fossils of at least five of the dinosaurs have been found together.

Gallery 5

Marginocephalia

Marginocephalians

Pachycephalosaurs

Ceratopsians

Marginocephalians

The name 'marginocephalia' means 'ridged shelf', as these dinosaurs all share very unusually shaped skulls. There were two main groups: the 'boneheaded' pachycephalosaurs, whose heads were in the shape of a dome, and the ceratopsians, which had long horns on their faces.

The pachycephalosaurs had small, bony ridges at the back of their skulls, while the ceratopsians had much larger, bony frills. Some certatopsians also had long horns jutting out from the top of their frills, as well as horns and spikes covering the tips of their noses and cheeks.

The pachycephalosaurs and early ceratopsians walked on two legs, but later ceratopsians walked on all fours. They were all plant-eaters, with simple, peg-like teeth and huge stomachs for digesting their food.

Marginocephalians first appeared in the Mid-Jurassic period but are mostly known from the Cretaceous. They lived in many different habitats, but most fossils have been found in Asia and western North America.

_____ *Key to plate* _____

1: Diabloceratops eatoni
Late Cretaceous, USA
Length: 5.5m; Weight: 2000kg
Discovered in 1998, this dinosaur may be an early ancestor of the famous *Triceratops* and has been given the name 'devil horn face'.

It was medium-sized, with a rounded nose and a skull that was covered with horns. It had two flat, bony crests extending along the top of its snout, long horns above its eyes and a small horn on its nose.

Like other ceratopsians, it was a plant eater, and it lived in an area covered in lakes and rivers, where it would have used its beaked mouth to feed on low-growing plants.

Pachycephalosaurs

Some of the most striking-looking dinosaurs appeared at the end of the Mesozoic era — including the pachycephalosaurs, with their incredibly thick skulls. Most pachycephalosaurs lived during the Late Cretaceous period in what is now North America and Asia. They were plant-eaters, with small weak arms, beaks for clipping off leaves and sharp, ridged teeth to help them chew.

Their most notable feature was their array of surprisingly shaped heads. They had thick domes on top of their skulls and a shelf at the back, dotted with bony lumps and spikes. We now know that their skulls became harder and thicker as the animal grew. Some species had skulls up to 23cm thick, which is 35 times thicker than a human's.

Pachycephalosaurs probably used their helmet-like heads either for display or to fight each other for mates or territory. They may have fought each other in fierce head butting contests, as mountain goats do today, or by pushing their heads into each other's sides, like male giraffes.

Key to plate

1: Stygimoloch spinifer
Late Cretaceous, USA
Length: 3m; Weight: 77kg
Stygimoloch's skull was covered in clusters of spikes. It looked very similar to *Dracorex*, but with shorter horns and a thicker dome.

2: Dracorex hogwartsia
Late Cretaceous, USA
Length: 2.4m; Weight: 45kg

This dinosaur's name means 'the dragon king of Hogwarts', inspired by its dragon-like appearance and the Harry Potter books.

3: Pachycephalosaurus wyomingensis
Late Cretaceous, USA
Length: 4.5m; Weight: 450kg
Pachycephalosaurus was the largest pachycephalosaur,

known only from its skull. It had a ring of bony spikes and an extremely thick dome.

4: Stegoceras validum
Late Cretaceous, N. America
Length: 2m; Weight: 40kg
Stegoceras was a goat-sized dinosaur and one of the first known pachycephalosaurs. It probably ate a varied diet of leaves, seeds, fruit and insects.

Ceratopsians

This group of dinosaurs are instantly recognisable by their spectacular neck frills and the long horns on their faces. They were plant-eaters, with a beak at the front of their mouths, and teeth well-suited for grinding up tough plants.

Early ceratopsians were much smaller, walked on two legs, and didn't have the enormous frills and spikes of their later relatives. But by the Late Cretaceous, all ceratopsians were walking on four legs and had developed an incredible variety of decorative frills and horns on their skulls. They may have used these horns to defend themselves against the theropods of the day or to signal to each other, in the same way stags use their antlers today.

We also know that many ceratopsians travelled in huge herds. Hundreds of these dinosaurs have been found together in what are known as 'bone beds' in the western United States. These herds would have provided protection against predators. Ceratopsians could have stampeded to ward off attackers or circled together, protecting the old and the young at the centre of the herd, much like the behaviour of modern elephants.

Key to plate

1: Psittacosaurus mongoliensis
Early Cretaceous, Asia
Length: 1.5m; Weight: 15kg
Psittacosaurus was an early ceratopsian with a pair of spikes jutting from its jaws. It also had hair-like bristles along its back.

2: Styracosaurus albertensis
Late Cretaceous, USA
Length: 5.5m; Weight: 3000kg
This ferocious-looking dinosaur had five spikes sprouting from its neck frill. These spikes were too weak to be used for fighting and were used to attract females.

3: Pentaceratops sternbergii
Late Cretaceous, USA
Length: 6.5m; Weight: 5000kg
This dinosaur's skull was up to 3m long, making it the longest skull of any land animal.

4: Triceratops horridus
Late Cretaceous, USA
Length: 9m; Weight: 11,000kg
As heavy as a truck, with three impressive horns on its face, *Triceratops* was a powerful beast – and it needed to be. *Tyrannosaurus* was a known predator and its tooth marks have been found on *Triceratops* skeletons.

Gallery 6

Non-Dinosaurs

Pterosaurs

Marine Reptiles

Mesozoic Mammals

Extinction

Pterosaurs

The pterosaurs were close cousins of the dinosaurs' and were the first animals, after insects, to take to the skies. They lived from the Late Triassic period to the end of the Cretaceous and their fossils have been found all over the world.

Pterosaur wings were made of a tough layer of skin and muscle, stretched between the ankle bone and an extremely long fourth finger. They had toothless bills and probably spent much of their lives soaring over oceans, diving for fish and scavenging for insects. Some were even successful land predators, walking, running and hunting on the ground.

Pterosaurs evolved into a diverse range of species, who ranged from the size of a pigeon to that of a small plane. Early pterosaurs were smaller, with long tails, while later species, which developed head crests, were the largest animals ever to fly.

Key to plate

1: Quetzalcoatlus northropi
Late Cretaceous, USA
Length: 12m;
Weight: uncertain
Quetzalcoatlus was one of the largest-known pterosaurs. It had a huge toothless beak and a wingspan the length of a bus.

2: Caiuajara dobruskii
Late Cretaceous, Brazil
Length: 2.4m;
Weight: uncertain
This species has only recently been discovered. It was found with 47 others of its kind, including both young and adults. It is thought Caiuajara lived in large groups, flew at a young age and had a head crest that changed shape as the animal grew.

3: Eudimorphodon ranzii
Late Triassic, Italy
Length: 1m; Weight: 10kg
Eudimorphodon was a typical early pterosaur, with a small wingspan, a short neck, sharp teeth and a long tail. It hunted for fish, catching them in its needle-like teeth.

4: Sordes pilosus
Late Jurassic, Kazakhstan
Length: 0.6m; Weight: 5kg
Sordes was the first pterosaur to be found covered in a fur-like coat, which it probably relied on for warmth.

5: Dimorphodon macronyx
Early Jurassic, England
Length: 1.2m; Weight: 12kg
This pterosaur had both fangs and grinding teeth, so it possibly ate a diet of insects and small animals. It was a poor flier that may only have made short flights.

Marine Reptiles

During the Mesozoic era, the seas were filled with a huge variety of reptiles, only very distantly related to the dinosaurs. They included the dolphin-like ichthyosaurs, which dominated the seas during the Late Triassic and Jurassic. The ichthyosaurs were well adapted to marine life, using their powerful tails and flippers to travel through the water. They had large eyes to help them see in murky depths and gave birth to live young in the water. However, they still needed to come to the surface to breathe.

Another dominant group of marine reptiles were the plesiosaurs. They had large lungs, to help them stay underwater for long periods of time, and two pairs of flippers, which they flapped like wings to 'fly' through the water. They had extremely long necks, small heads and sharp, pointed teeth for catching fish.

The pliosaurs were the top underwater predators of their time. They were true sea monsters with huge heads and massive, incredibly strong jaws. Their prey included large fish, ichthyosaurs, plesiosaurs and even dinosaurs they scavenged from the shore.

--- *Key to plate* ---

1: Nothosaurus marchicus
Middle Triassic, Holland
Length: 1.5–2m; Weight: 80kg
Nothosaurus belonged to a group called the nothosaurs, which date from the same time as the first dinosaurs. They probably lived like seals, breeding on beaches and diving into the sea to feed.

2: Ichthyosaurus communis
Early Jurassic, England
Length: 2m; Weight: 90kg
Ichthyosaurus was a fast hunter that caught fish in its needle-sharp teeth.

3: Elasmosaurus platyurus
Late Cretaceous, USA
Length: 14m; Weight: 2000kg
This plesiosaur was one of the longest-necked creatures ever to have lived.

4: Kronosaurus queenslandicus
Early Cretaceous, Australia
Length: 10m; Weight: 11,000kg
Kronosaurus was a pliosaur with a massive skull and short, muscular neck. It fed on turtles and plesiosaurs.

5: Tylosaurus proriger
Late Cretaceous, USA
Length: 14m;
Weight: uncertain
Tylosaurus was a type of mosasaur. It was a deadly predator with double rows of pointed teeth.

Mesozoic Mammals

The first mammals (warm-blooded animals) evolved in the Triassic period from mammal-like reptiles known as cynodonts. Early mammals were small, covered in fur and mainly fed on insects. Like their reptile ancestors, they laid eggs, rather than giving birth to live young, and may well have hunted at night.

From these small beginnings, the mammals of the Mesozoic began to develop into many different forms. Some ate both meat and plants, some adapted to life in the water, while others lived on the ground or in trees.

Exciting new discoveries in China have also revealed that some mammals from the Cretaceous period were much larger than previously thought, reaching lengths of one metre or more, and even preying on baby dinosaurs.

Key to plate

1: Repenomamus giganticus
Early Cretaceous, China
Length: 1m; Weight: 14kg
Repenomamus was a raccoon-like animal, much bigger than other mammals from this time. One was found with a young *Psittacosaurus* in its gut.

2: Cynognathus crateronotus
Early–Mid Triassic, Africa, South America, Antarctica
Length: 1.2m; Weight: 6.5kg
A fast, fierce predator, *Cynognathus* had wide jaws and sharp teeth for slicing through flesh.

3: Megazostrodon
Late Triassic–Early Jurassic, South Africa
Length: 10cm; Weight: 28g
Megazostrodon was a tiny creature and most of its body length was made up by its tail. It probably lived in underground tunnels and may have eaten roots or insects.

4: Eomaia scansoria
Early Cretaceous, China
Length: 14cm; Weight: 20–25g
Its name means 'dawn mother' as it is the earliest-known ancestor of placental mammals, which means it gave birth to live young, rather than laying eggs.

5: Volaticotherium antiquum
Mid–Late Jurassic, China
Length: 30.5cm; Weight: uncertain
This animal had long, grasping toes and a flap of skin between its legs. It would have been able to climb trees and then glide between the branches, much like a flying squirrel today.

Extinction

Around 66 million years ago, the Mesozoic era ended in a mass extinction. This huge catastrophe wiped out the dinosaurs and more than half the world's animal species, including mosasaurs, plesiosaurs, pterosaurs and much of the world's plants.

Scientists believe the extinction was caused by an asteroid, a large rock from space, colliding with the Earth. Its impact would have led to wildfires, huge waves and clouds of dust that blocked out the sunlight for years. As the plants withered and died, so too did the plant-eaters, which in turn starved the meat-eaters. But some types of animals somehow survived, including small lizards, snakes, birds, insects, mammals, sharks, turtles, amphibians and crocodiles.

For the survivors, the extinction was an opportunity. Birds spread around the world and mammals crept out from the undergrowth and evolved into a spectacular variety of forms, including the whale-like *Dorudon* and the tiny ancestor of modern horses, *Hyracotherium*. By the end of the Palaeogene period that followed, 23 million years later, there were primates, horses, bats, dogs, pigs, cats and whales. The 'Age of Mammals' had begun.

Key to plate

1: Dorudon
Palaeocene, N. America, Africa
Length: 5m; Weight: 450kg
Dorudon was an ancient whale that fed on fish and molluscs.

2: Palaeotrionyx
Palaeocene, N. America
Length: 45cm; Weight: 6kg
Palaeotrionyx was a soft-shelled turtle, with a long neck and sharp beak.

3: Moeritherium
Eocene, Africa
Length: 70cm; Weight: 235kg
A pig-like mammal related to elephants, *Moeritherium* lived in swamps and rivers.

4: Hyracotherium
Eocene, N. America & Europe
Length: 78cm; Weight: 9kg
The ancestor of modern horses, *Hyracotherium* lived

around 50 million years ago and fed on soft plants.

5: Gastornis
Late Palaeocene & Eocene, Europe, China & possibly USA
Height: 2m; Weight: 170kg
Gastornis was a large, flightless bird with a powerful beak.

Glossary

Allosauroidea A family of meat-eating theropod dinosaurs from the Late Jurassic period.

Ankylosaurs A group of plant-eating, four-legged dinosaurs covered in bony plates and spikes.

Archosaurs An ancient group of reptiles that includes dinosaurs, pterosaurs, crocodiles and their relatives.

Camouflage Colours or patterns that help an animal to blend in with its surroundings and hide from predators.

Carcharodontosauridae A group of meat-eating theropod dinosaurs known from Africa and South America.

Carnivore An animal that eats meat.

Ceratopsians A group of plant-eating, four-legged dinosaurs. Most had bony frills at the back of their necks and horns on their faces.

Coelurosauria A group of theropod dinosaurs that are closely related to modern birds.

Cretaceous The third period of the Mesozoic era, lasting from 145 to 66 million years ago.

Dromaeosaurids A group of meat-eating, feathered dinosaurs, very closely related to modern birds.

Evolution The process by which living things change over time.

Extinct A species of animal or plant that no longer has any living members.

Fossil The remains of a dead plant or animal, preserved in rock.

Herbivore An animal that eats plants.

Ichthyosaurs A group of dolphin-like marine reptiles that lived during the Mesozoic era.

Jurassic The second period of the Mesozoic era, lasting from 201 to 145 million years ago.

Mammals A group of warm-blooded, often hairy animals that give milk to their young.

Marginocephalians A group of dinosaurs with a bony shelf at the back of their skulls.

Mesozoic era A period of time lasting from 252 to 66 million years ago. It is divided into three periods: the Triassic, the Jurassic and the Cretaceous.

Omnivore An animal that eats a variety of plants and animals.

Ornithischians One of the two main groups of dinosaurs, with hip bones similar to those of modern birds.

Ornithopods A group of plant-eating, ornithischian dinosaurs with horny beaks.

Pachycephalosaurs A group of thick-skulled, ornithischian dinosaurs that walked on two legs.

Plesiosaurs Marine reptiles that lived during the Mesozoic era. They had short tails and four flippers.

Pliosaurs A group of plesiosaurs with short, thick necks, huge heads and crocodile-like teeth.

Predators Animals that hunt and eat other animals for food.

Pterosaurs Flying reptiles that lived during the Mesozoic era.

Reptiles A group of cold-blooded animals, including turtles, lizards, crocodiles, pterosaurs and dinosaurs.

Saurischians One of the two main groups of dinosaurs, with hip bones similar to modern lizards.

Sauropodomorphs A group of saurischian, mostly plant-eating dinosaurs, with long necks and tails.

Sauropods This group of plant-eating saurischian dinosaurs included the largest animals ever to walk the earth.

Species A particular type of plant, animal or other living thing.

Stegosaurs One of the groups of armoured dinosaurs with bony plates and spines on their backs.

Theropods A group of saurischian dinosaurs that walked on two legs. Most theropods were meat-eaters.

Thyreophorans A group of ornithischian dinosaurs that walked on four legs and had bony plates or spikes on their bodies. This group includes the stegosaurs and ankylosaurs.

Triassic The first period of the Mesozoic era, lasting from 252 to 201 million years ago.

Index